These cleaning Checklists Belong to

_____

IDEAS TO DECLUTTER YOUR HOME

Living Room

- [ ] Old magazines and newspapers
- [ ] CDs and DVDs
- [ ] Books
- [ ] Unused vases and dried flowers
- [ ] Photos with no sentimental value
- [ ] Letters
- [ ] Old cellphones & electronic devices
- [ ] Catalogs
- [ ] Throw pillows & blankets
- [ ] Souvenirs you don't need
- [ ] Computer cords and chargers
- [ ] Knickknacks & ornaments
- [ ]
- [ ]

Kitchen

- [ ] Pots and Pans
- [ ] Broken or Incomplete Dishes
- [ ] Extra coffee mugs & glasses
- [ ] Recipes & cookbooks never used
- [ ] Expired foods
- [ ] Extra containers and jars
- [ ] Plastic shopping bags
- [ ] Broken & duplicate small apliances
- [ ] Kitchen gadgets not used
- [ ] Extra dishcloths and towels
- [ ] Extra potholders
- [ ] Duplicate not needed products
- [ ]
- [ ]

Bathroom

- [ ] Old makeup
- [ ] Old towels
- [ ] Old washcloths
- [ ] Old bathmats
- [ ] Expired medicines
- [ ] Old tothbrushes
- [ ] Old toiletries
- [ ] Hair products not used
- [ ] Old nail polish
- [ ] Old brushes
- [ ] Nearly gone bars of soap
- [ ] Nearly empty cleaning products
- [ ]
- [ ]

Bedrooms

- [ ] Old sheets & bedding
- [ ] Old pillows
- [ ] T shirts you don't wear
- [ ] Clothes that are too small
- [ ] Clothing not worn in 2 years
- [ ] Clothing you don't like
- [ ] Purses you don't use
- [ ] Sweatpants that are threadbare
- [ ] Displayed photos can go in albums
- [ ] Old paperwork
- [ ] Old bank statements
- [ ] Old paper bills
- [ ]
- [ ]

Kids Stuff

- [ ] Unused outside toys
- [ ] Not needed kids art and papers
- [ ] Toys not used
- [ ] Broken toys
- [ ] Clothes that are too small
- [ ] Shoes that don't fit
- [ ] Extra Lego blocks and crayons
- [ ] Outgrown books
- [ ] Old toothbrushes
- [ ] DVDs not watched
- [ ] Old school assignments
- [ ] Old greeting cards & invitations
- [ ]
- [ ]

Misc

- [ ] Packaging from purchases
- [ ] Instruction booklets & manuals
- [ ] Things you haven't missed
- [ ] Unfinished craft projects
- [ ] Half empty paint containers
- [ ] Junk mail
- [ ] Sports equipment not used
- [ ] Tangled jewelry
- [ ] Unused garden equipment
- [ ] Expired coupons
- [ ] Extra coat hangers
- [ ] Things that don't make you happ
- [ ]
- [ ]

Cleaning Checklist

MONTH: _____

KITCHEN	NUMBER OF TIMES						
	1	2	3	4	5	6	7
Mop							
Dust							
Wipe Cabinets							
Wipe Outside of Appliances							
Clean Inside of Microwave							
Clean Kitchen Sink							
Clean inside of refrigerator							
Clean inside of stove							
Dust light fixtures							
Clean blinds and curtains							
Wipe doors and baseboards							

DAILY TASKS FOCUS	
Wipe Counters & Stovetop	
Sweep	
Take out trash	
Do Dishes	

SUPPLIES TO PURCHASE

Cleaning Checklist

MONTH: _____

LIVING ROOM & DINNING ROOM	NUMBER OF TIMES						
	1	2	3	4	5	6	7
Vacuum							
Dust furniture							
Dust Pictures							
Dust light fixtures							
Clean blinds, curtains, drapes							
Clean inside windows							
Wipe windowsils							
Wipe baseboards & light switchplates							
Shampoo carpet							

DAILY TASKS FOCUS	
Clean up clutter	
Tidy magazines	
Fluff sofa pillows	

SUPPLIES TO PURCHASE

Cleaning Checklist

MONTH: _____

BATHROOM & LAUNDRY	NUMBER OF TIMES						
	1	2	3	4	5	6	7
Clean facebowl and counter							
Clean shower							
Wipe shower curtains/door							
Clean bathtub							
Clean mirrors & light fixtures							
Vacuum							
Mop							
Dust							
Wipe Cabinets & baseboards							
Empty trash							
Wash clothes							
Wash bedding							
Wash bath towels & cloths							

DAILY TASKS FOCUS

SUPPLIES TO PURCHASE

Cleaning Checklist

MONTH: _____

BEDROOM	NUMBER OF TIMES						
	1	2	3	4	5	6	7
Make Beds							
Hang up clothes							
Fold and put away clothes							
Tidy room							
Dust furniture							
Dust light fixtures and switchplates							
Vacuum							
Tidy drawers							
Tidy bookshelves							
Empty Trash							
Declutter desk							
Clean out closet							
Discard old paperwork							

DAILY TASKS FOCUS

SUPPLIES TO PURCHASE

Cleaning Checklist

MONTH: _____

BEDROOM	Number of Times						
	1	2	3	4	5	6	7
Make Beds							
Hang up clothes							
Fold and put away clothes							
Tidy room							
Dust furniture							
Dust light fixtures and switchplates							
Vacuum							
Tidy drawers							
Tidy bookshelves							
Empty Trash							
Declutter desk							
Clean out closet							
Discard old paperwork							

DAILY TASKS FOCUS

SUPPLIES TO PURCHASE

Cleaning Checklist

MONTH: _____

BEDROOM	NUMBER OF TIMES						
	1	2	3	4	5	6	7
Make Beds							
Hang up clothes							
Fold and put away clothes							
Tidy room							
Dust furniture							
Dust light fixtures and switchplates							
Vacuum							
Tidy drawers							
Tidy bookshelves							
Empty Trash							
Declutter desk							
Clean out closet							
Discard old paperwork							

DAILY TASKS FOCUS	

SUPPLIES TO PURCHASE

Cleaning Checklist

MONTH: _____

BEDROOM	NUMBER OF TIMES						
	1	2	3	4	5	6	7
Make Beds							
Hang up clothes							
Fold and put away clothes							
Tidy room							
Dust furniture							
Dust light fixtures and switchplates							
Vacuum							
Tidy drawers							
Tidy bookshelves							
Empty Trash							
Declutter desk							
Clean out closet							
Discard old paperwork							

DAILY TASKS FOCUS

SUPPLIES TO PURCHASE

Kids Chores

NAME: _____

CHORES	NUMBER OF TIMES						
	SUN	MON	TU	WED	THU	FRI	SAT

NOTES

Cleaning Checklist

MONTH: _____

ADDITIONAL CLEANING	NUMBER OF TIMES						
	1	2	3	4	5	6	7

TASKS FOCUS	

SUPPLIES TO PURCHASE

Cleaning Checklist

MONTH: _____

KITCHEN	NUMBER OF TIMES						
	1	2	3	4	5	6	7
Mop							
Dust							
Wipe Cabinets							
Wipe Outside of Appliances							
Clean Inside of Microwave							
Clean Kitchen Sink							
Clean inside of refrigerator							
Clean inside of stove							
Dust light fixtures							
Clean blinds and curtains							
Wipe doors and baseboards							

DAILY TASKS FOCUS	
Wipe Counters & Stovetop	
Sweep	
Take out trash	
Do Dishes	

SUPPLIES TO PURCHASE

Cleaning Checklist

MONTH: _____

LIVING ROOM & DINNING ROOM	NUMBER OF TIMES						
	1	2	3	4	5	6	7
Vacuum							
Dust furniture							
Dust Pictures							
Dust light fixtures							
Clean blinds, curtains, drapes							
Clean inside windows							
Wipe windowsils							
Wipe baseboards & light switchplates							
Shampoo carpet							

DAILY TASKS FOCUS	
Clean up clutter	
Tidy magazines	
Fluff sofa pillows	

SUPPLIES TO PURCHASE

Cleaning Checklist

MONTH: _____

BATHROOM & LAUNDRY	NUMBER OF TIMES						
	1	2	3	4	5	6	7
Clean facebowl and counter							
Clean shower							
Wipe shower curtains/door							
Clean bathtub							
Clean mirrors & light fixtures							
Vacuum							
Mop							
Dust							
Wipe Cabinets & baseboards							
Empty trash							
Wash clothes							
Wash bedding							
Wash bath towels & cloths							

DAILY TASKS FOCUS

SUPPLIES TO PURCHASE

Cleaning Checklist

MONTH: _____

BEDROOM	NUMBER OF TIMES						
	1	2	3	4	5	6	7
Make Beds							
Hang up clothes							
Fold and put away clothes							
Tidy room							
Dust furniture							
Dust light fixtures and switchplates							
Vacuum							
Tidy drawers							
Tidy bookshelves							
Empty Trash							
Declutter desk							
Clean out closet							
Discard old paperwork							

DAILY TASKS FOCUS

SUPPLIES TO PURCHASE

Cleaning Checklist

MONTH: _____

BEDROOM	NUMBER OF TIMES						
	1	2	3	4	5	6	7
Make Beds							
Hang up clothes							
Fold and put away clothes							
Tidy room							
Dust furniture							
Dust light fixtures and switchplates							
Vacuum							
Tidy drawers							
Tidy bookshelves							
Empty Trash							
Declutter desk							
Clean out closet							
Discard old paperwork							

DAILY TASKS FOCUS

SUPPLIES TO PURCHASE

Cleaning Checklist

MONTH: _____

BEDROOM	NUMBER OF TIMES						
	1	2	3	4	5	6	7
Make Beds							
Hang up clothes							
Fold and put away clothes							
Tidy room							
Dust furniture							
Dust light fixtures and switchplates							
Vacuum							
Tidy drawers							
Tidy bookshelves							
Empty Trash							
Declutter desk							
Clean out closet							
Discard old paperwork							

DAILY TASKS FOCUS

SUPPLIES TO PURCHASE

Cleaning Checklist

MONTH: _____

BEDROOM	NUMBER OF TIMES						
	1	2	3	4	5	6	7
Make Beds							
Hang up clothes							
Fold and put away clothes							
Tidy room							
Dust furniture							
Dust light fixtures and switchplates							
Vacuum							
Tidy drawers							
Tidy bookshelves							
Empty Trash							
Declutter desk							
Clean out closet							
Discard old paperwork							

DAILY TASKS FOCUS

SUPPLIES TO PURCHASE

Kids Chores

NAME: _____

CHORES	SUN	MON	Number of Times				
			TU	WED	THU	FRI	SAT

NOTES

Cleaning Checklist

MONTH: _____

ADDITIONAL CLEANING	NUMBER OF TIMES						
	1	2	3	4	5	6	7

TASKS FOCUS	

SUPPLIES TO PURCHASE

Cleaning Checklist

MONTH: _____

KITCHEN	NUMBER OF TIMES						
	1	2	3	4	5	6	7
Mop							
Dust							
Wipe Cabinets							
Wipe Outside of Appliances							
Clean Inside of Microwave							
Clean Kitchen Sink							
Clean inside of refrigerator							
Clean inside of stove							
Dust light fixtures							
Clean blinds and curtains							
Wipe doors and baseboards							

DAILY TASKS FOCUS	
Wipe Counters & Stovetop	
Sweep	
Take out trash	
Do Dishes	

SUPPLIES TO PURCHASE

Cleaning Checklist

LIVING ROOM & DINNING ROOM	NUMBER OF TIMES						
	1	2	3	4	5	6	7
Vacuum							
Dust furniture							
Dust Pictures							
Dust light fixtures							
Clean blinds, curtains, drapes							
Clean inside windows							
Wipe windowsils							
Wipe baseboards & light switchplates							
Shampoo carpet							

DAILY TASKS FOCUS	
Clean up clutter	
Tidy magazines	
Fluff sofa pillows	

SUPPLIES TO PURCHASE

Cleaning Checklist

MONTH: _____

BATHROOM & LAUNDRY	NUMBER OF TIMES						
	1	2	3	4	5	6	7
Clean facebowl and counter							
Clean shower							
Wipe shower curtains/door							
Clean bathtub							
Clean mirrors & light fixtures							
Vacuum							
Mop							
Dust							
Wipe Cabinets & baseboards							
Empty trash							
Wash clothes							
Wash bedding							
Wash bath towels & cloths							

DAILY TASKS FOCUS

SUPPLIES TO PURCHASE

Cleaning Checklist

MONTH: _____

BEDROOM	NUMBER OF TIMES						
	1	2	3	4	5	6	7
Make Beds							
Hang up clothes							
Fold and put away clothes							
Tidy room							
Dust furniture							
Dust light fixtures and switchplates							
Vacuum							
Tidy drawers							
Tidy bookshelves							
Empty Trash							
Declutter desk							
Clean out closet							
Discard old paperwork							

DAILY TASKS FOCUS	

SUPPLIES TO PURCHASE

Cleaning Checklist

MONTH: _____

BEDROOM	NUMBER OF TIMES						
	1	2	3	4	5	6	7
Make Beds							
Hang up clothes							
Fold and put away clothes							
Tidy room							
Dust furniture							
Dust light fixtures and switchplates							
Vacuum							
Tidy drawers							
Tidy bookshelves							
Empty Trash							
Declutter desk							
Clean out closet							
Discard old paperwork							

DAILY TASKS FOCUS

SUPPLIES TO PURCHASE

Cleaning Checklist

MONTH: _____

BEDROOM	NUMBER OF TIMES						
	1	2	3	4	5	6	7
Make Beds							
Hang up clothes							
Fold and put away clothes							
Tidy room							
Dust furniture							
Dust light fixtures and switchplates							
Vacuum							
Tidy drawers							
Tidy bookshelves							
Empty Trash							
Declutter desk							
Clean out closet							
Discard old paperwork							

DAILY TASKS FOCUS

SUPPLIES TO PURCHASE

Cleaning Checklist

MONTH: _____

BEDROOM	Number of Times						
	1	2	3	4	5	6	7
Make Beds							
Hang up clothes							
Fold and put away clothes							
Tidy room							
Dust furniture							
Dust light fixtures and switchplates							
Vacuum							
Tidy drawers							
Tidy bookshelves							
Empty Trash							
Declutter desk							
Clean out closet							
Discard old paperwork							

DAILY TASKS FOCUS

SUPPLIES TO PURCHASE

Kids Chores

NAME: _____

CHORES	NUMBER OF TIMES						
	SUN	MON	TU	WED	THU	FRI	SAT

NOTES

Cleaning Checklist

MONTH: _____

ADDITIONAL CLEANING	NUMBER OF TIMES						
	1	2	3	4	5	6	7

TASKS FOCUS	

SUPPLIES TO PURCHASE

Cleaning Checklist

MONTH: _____

KITCHEN	NUMBER OF TIMES						
	1	2	3	4	5	6	7
Mop							
Dust							
Wipe Cabinets							
Wipe Outside of Appliances							
Clean Inside of Microwave							
Clean Kitchen Sink							
Clean inside of refrigerator							
Clean inside of stove							
Dust light fixtures							
Clean blinds and curtains							
Wipe doors and baseboards							

DAILY TASKS FOCUS	
Wipe Counters & Stovetop	
Sweep	
Take out trash	
Do Dishes	

SUPPLIES TO PURCHASE

Cleaning Checklist

LIVING ROOM & DINNING ROOM	NUMBER OF TIMES						
	1	2	3	4	5	6	7
Vacuum							
Dust furniture							
Dust Pictures							
Dust light fixtures							
Clean blinds, curtains, drapes							
Clean inside windows							
Wipe windowsils							
Wipe baseboards & light switchplates							
Shampoo carpet							

DAILY TASKS FOCUS	
Clean up clutter	
Tidy magazines	
Fluff sofa pillows	

SUPPLIES TO PURCHASE

Cleaning Checklist

MONTH: _____

BATHROOM & LAUNDRY	NUMBER OF TIMES						
	1	2	3	4	5	6	7
Clean facebowl and counter							
Clean shower							
Wipe shower curtains/door							
Clean bathtub							
Clean mirrors & light fixtures							
Vacuum							
Mop							
Dust							
Wipe Cabinets & baseboards							
Empty trash							
Wash clothes							
Wash bedding							
Wash bath towels & cloths							

DAILY TASKS FOCUS

SUPPLIES TO PURCHASE

Cleaning Checklist

MONTH: _____

BEDROOM	NUMBER OF TIMES						
	1	2	3	4	5	6	7
Make Beds							
Hang up clothes							
Fold and put away clothes							
Tidy room							
Dust furniture							
Dust light fixtures and switchplates							
Vacuum							
Tidy drawers							
Tidy bookshelves							
Empty Trash							
Declutter desk							
Clean out closet							
Discard old paperwork							

DAILY TASKS FOCUS

SUPPLIES TO PURCHASE

Cleaning Checklist

MONTH: _____

BEDROOM	NUMBER OF TIMES						
	1	2	3	4	5	6	7
Make Beds							
Hang up clothes							
Fold and put away clothes							
Tidy room							
Dust furniture							
Dust light fixtures and switchplates							
Vacuum							
Tidy drawers							
Tidy bookshelves							
Empty Trash							
Declutter desk							
Clean out closet							
Discard old paperwork							

DAILY TASKS FOCUS

SUPPLIES TO PURCHASE

Cleaning Checklist

MONTH: _____

BEDROOM	NUMBER OF TIMES						
	1	2	3	4	5	6	7
Make Beds							
Hang up clothes							
Fold and put away clothes							
Tidy room							
Dust furniture							
Dust light fixtures and switchplates							
Vacuum							
Tidy drawers							
Tidy bookshelves							
Empty Trash							
Declutter desk							
Clean out closet							
Discard old paperwork							

DAILY TASKS FOCUS	

SUPPLIES TO PURCHASE

Cleaning Checklist

MONTH: _____

BEDROOM	Number of Times						
	1	2	3	4	5	6	7
Make Beds							
Hang up clothes							
Fold and put away clothes							
Tidy room							
Dust furniture							
Dust light fixtures and switchplates							
Vacuum							
Tidy drawers							
Tidy bookshelves							
Empty Trash							
Declutter desk							
Clean out closet							
Discard old paperwork							

DAILY TASKS FOCUS	

SUPPLIES TO PURCHASE

Kids Chores

NAME: _____

CHORES	NUMBER OF TIMES						
	SUN	MON	TU	WED	THU	FRI	SAT

NOTES

Cleaning Checklist

MONTH: _____

ADDITIONAL CLEANING

	NUMBER OF TIMES						
	1	2	3	4	5	6	7

TASKS FOCUS

SUPPLIES TO PURCHASE

Cleaning Checklist

MONTH: _____

KITCHEN	NUMBER OF TIMES						
	1	2	3	4	5	6	7
Mop							
Dust							
Wipe Cabinets							
Wipe Outside of Appliances							
Clean Inside of Microwave							
Clean Kitchen Sink							
Clean inside of refrigerator							
Clean inside of stove							
Dust light fixtures							
Clean blinds and curtains							
Wipe doors and baseboards							

DAILY TASKS FOCUS	
Wipe Counters & Stovetop	
Sweep	
Take out trash	
Do Dishes	

SUPPLIES TO PURCHASE

Cleaning Checklist

MONTH: _____

LIVING ROOM & DINNING ROOM	NUMBER OF TIMES						
	1	2	3	4	5	6	7
Vacuum							
Dust furniture							
Dust Pictures							
Dust light fixtures							
Clean blinds, curtains, drapes							
Clean inside windows							
Wipe windowsils							
Wipe baseboards & light switchplates							
Shampoo carpet							

DAILY TASKS FOCUS	
Clean up clutter	
Tidy magazines	
Fluff sofa pillows	

SUPPLIES TO PURCHASE

Cleaning Checklist

MONTH: _____

BATHROOM & LAUNDRY	NUMBER OF TIMES						
	1	2	3	4	5	6	7
Clean facebowl and counter							
Clean shower							
Wipe shower curtains/door							
Clean bathtub							
Clean mirrors & light fixtures							
Vacuum							
Mop							
Dust							
Wipe Cabinets & baseboards							
Empty trash							
Wash clothes							
Wash bedding							
Wash bath towels & cloths							

DAILY TASKS FOCUS

SUPPLIES TO PURCHASE

Cleaning Checklist

MONTH: _____

BEDROOM	NUMBER OF TIMES						
	1	2	3	4	5	6	7
Make Beds							
Hang up clothes							
Fold and put away clothes							
Tidy room							
Dust furniture							
Dust light fixtures and switchplates							
Vacuum							
Tidy drawers							
Tidy bookshelves							
Empty Trash							
Declutter desk							
Clean out closet							
Discard old paperwork							

DAILY TASKS FOCUS

SUPPLIES TO PURCHASE

Cleaning Checklist

MONTH: _____

BEDROOM	NUMBER OF TIMES						
	1	2	3	4	5	6	7
Make Beds							
Hang up clothes							
Fold and put away clothes							
Tidy room							
Dust furniture							
Dust light fixtures and switchplates							
Vacuum							
Tidy drawers							
Tidy bookshelves							
Empty Trash							
Declutter desk							
Clean out closet							
Discard old paperwork							

DAILY TASKS FOCUS	

SUPPLIES TO PURCHASE

Cleaning Checklist

MONTH: _____

BEDROOM	NUMBER OF TIMES						
	1	2	3	4	5	6	7
Make Beds							
Hang up clothes							
Fold and put away clothes							
Tidy room							
Dust furniture							
Dust light fixtures and switchplates							
Vacuum							
Tidy drawers							
Tidy bookshelves							
Empty Trash							
Declutter desk							
Clean out closet							
Discard old paperwork							

DAILY TASKS FOCUS

SUPPLIES TO PURCHASE

Cleaning Checklist

MONTH: _____

BEDROOM	Number of Times						
	1	2	3	4	5	6	7
Make Beds							
Hang up clothes							
Fold and put away clothes							
Tidy room							
Dust furniture							
Dust light fixtures and switchplates							
Vacuum							
Tidy drawers							
Tidy bookshelves							
Empty Trash							
Declutter desk							
Clean out closet							
Discard old paperwork							

DAILY TASKS FOCUS

SUPPLIES TO PURCHASE

Kids Chores

NAME: _____

CHORES	NUMBER OF TIMES						
	SUN	MON	TU	WED	THU	FRI	SAT

		NOTES

Cleaning Checklist

MONTH: _____

ADDITIONAL CLEANING	NUMBER OF TIMES						
	1	2	3	4	5	6	7

TASKS FOCUS	

SUPPLIES TO PURCHASE

Cleaning Checklist

MONTH: _____

KITCHEN	NUMBER OF TIMES						
	1	2	3	4	5	6	7
Mop							
Dust							
Wipe Cabinets							
Wipe Outside of Appliances							
Clean Inside of Microwave							
Clean Kitchen Sink							
Clean inside of refrigerator							
Clean inside of stove							
Dust light fixtures							
Clean blinds and curtains							
Wipe doors and baseboards							

DAILY TASKS FOCUS	
Wipe Counters & Stovetop	
Sweep	
Take out trash	
Do Dishes	

SUPPLIES TO PURCHASE

Cleaning Checklist

MONTH: _____

LIVING ROOM & DINNING ROOM	NUMBER OF TIMES						
	1	2	3	4	5	6	7
Vacuum							
Dust furniture							
Dust Pictures							
Dust light fixtures							
Clean blinds, curtains, drapes							
Clean inside windows							
Wipe windowsils							
Wipe baseboards & light switchplates							
Shampoo carpet							

DAILY TASKS FOCUS	
Clean up clutter	
Tidy magazines	
Fluff sofa pillows	

SUPPLIES TO PURCHASE

Cleaning Checklist

MONTH: _____

BATHROOM & LAUNDRY	NUMBER OF TIMES						
	1	2	3	4	5	6	7
Clean facebowl and counter							
Clean shower							
Wipe shower curtains/door							
Clean bathtub							
Clean mirrors & light fixtures							
Vacuum							
Mop							
Dust							
Wipe Cabinets & baseboards							
Empty trash							
Wash clothes							
Wash bedding							
Wash bath towels & cloths							

DAILY TASKS FOCUS	

SUPPLIES TO PURCHASE

Cleaning Checklist

MONTH: _____

BEDROOM	NUMBER OF TIMES						
	1	2	3	4	5	6	7
Make Beds							
Hang up clothes							
Fold and put away clothes							
Tidy room							
Dust furniture							
Dust light fixtures and switchplates							
Vacuum							
Tidy drawers							
Tidy bookshelves							
Empty Trash							
Declutter desk							
Clean out closet							
Discard old paperwork							

DAILY TASKS FOCUS	

SUPPLIES TO PURCHASE

Cleaning Checklist

MONTH: _____

BEDROOM	NUMBER OF TIMES						
	1	2	3	4	5	6	7
Make Beds							
Hang up clothes							
Fold and put away clothes							
Tidy room							
Dust furniture							
Dust light fixtures and switchplates							
Vacuum							
Tidy drawers							
Tidy bookshelves							
Empty Trash							
Declutter desk							
Clean out closet							
Discard old paperwork							

DAILY TASKS FOCUS

SUPPLIES TO PURCHASE

Cleaning Checklist

MONTH: _____

BEDROOM	NUMBER OF TIMES						
	1	2	3	4	5	6	7
Make Beds							
Hang up clothes							
Fold and put away clothes							
Tidy room							
Dust furniture							
Dust light fixtures and switchplates							
Vacuum							
Tidy drawers							
Tidy bookshelves							
Empty Trash							
Declutter desk							
Clean out closet							
Discard old paperwork							

DAILY TASKS FOCUS	

SUPPLIES TO PURCHASE

Cleaning Checklist

MONTH: _____

BEDROOM	NUMBER OF TIMES						
	1	2	3	4	5	6	7
Make Beds							
Hang up clothes							
Fold and put away clothes							
Tidy room							
Dust furniture							
Dust light fixtures and switchplates							
Vacuum							
Tidy drawers							
Tidy bookshelves							
Empty Trash							
Declutter desk							
Clean out closet							
Discard old paperwork							

DAILY TASKS FOCUS

SUPPLIES TO PURCHASE

Kids Chores

NAME: _____

CHORES	Number of Times						
	SUN	MON	TU	WED	THU	FRI	SAT

NOTES

Cleaning Checklist

MONTH: _____

ADDITIONAL CLEANING	NUMBER OF TIMES						
	1	2	3	4	5	6	7

TASKS FOCUS	

SUPPLIES TO PURCHASE

Cleaning Checklist

MONTH: _____

NUMBER OF TIMES

KITCHEN	1	2	3	4	5	6	7
Mop							
Dust							
Wipe Cabinets							
Wipe Outside of Appliances							
Clean Inside of Microwave							
Clean Kitchen Sink							
Clean inside of refrigerator							
Clean inside of stove							
Dust light fixtures							
Clean blinds and curtains							
Wipe doors and baseboards							

DAILY TASKS FOCUS	
Wipe Counters & Stovetop	
Sweep	
Take out trash	
Do Dishes	

SUPPLIES TO PURCHASE

Cleaning Checklist

MONTH: _____

LIVING ROOM & DINNING ROOM	NUMBER OF TIMES						
	1	2	3	4	5	6	7
Vacuum							
Dust furniture							
Dust Pictures							
Dust light fixtures							
Clean blinds, curtains, drapes							
Clean inside windows							
Wipe windowsils							
Wipe baseboards & light switchplates							
Shampoo carpet							

DAILY TASKS FOCUS	
Clean up clutter	
Tidy magazines	
Fluff sofa pillows	

SUPPLIES TO PURCHASE

Cleaning Checklist

MONTH: _____

BATHROOM & LAUNDRY	NUMBER OF TIMES						
	1	2	3	4	5	6	7
Clean facebowl and counter							
Clean shower							
Wipe shower curtains/door							
Clean bathtub							
Clean mirrors & light fixtures							
Vacuum							
Mop							
Dust							
Wipe Cabinets & baseboards							
Empty trash							
Wash clothes							
Wash bedding							
Wash bath towels & cloths							

DAILY TASKS FOCUS	

SUPPLIES TO PURCHASE

Cleaning Checklist

MONTH: _____

BEDROOM	Number of Times						
	1	2	3	4	5	6	7
Make Beds							
Hang up clothes							
Fold and put away clothes							
Tidy room							
Dust furniture							
Dust light fixtures and switchplates							
Vacuum							
Tidy drawers							
Tidy bookshelves							
Empty Trash							
Declutter desk							
Clean out closet							
Discard old paperwork							

DAILY TASKS FOCUS	

SUPPLIES TO PURCHASE

Cleaning Checklist

MONTH: _____

BEDROOM	NUMBER OF TIMES						
	1	2	3	4	5	6	7
Make Beds							
Hang up clothes							
Fold and put away clothes							
Tidy room							
Dust furniture							
Dust light fixtures and switchplates							
Vacuum							
Tidy drawers							
Tidy bookshelves							
Empty Trash							
Declutter desk							
Clean out closet							
Discard old paperwork							

DAILY TASKS FOCUS

SUPPLIES TO PURCHASE

Cleaning Checklist

MONTH: _____

BEDROOM	NUMBER OF TIMES						
	1	2	3	4	5	6	7
Make Beds							
Hang up clothes							
Fold and put away clothes							
Tidy room							
Dust furniture							
Dust light fixtures and switchplates							
Vacuum							
Tidy drawers							
Tidy bookshelves							
Empty Trash							
Declutter desk							
Clean out closet							
Discard old paperwork							

DAILY TASKS FOCUS

SUPPLIES TO PURCHASE

Cleaning Checklist

MONTH: _____

BEDROOM	NUMBER OF TIMES						
	1	2	3	4	5	6	7
Make Beds							
Hang up clothes							
Fold and put away clothes							
Tidy room							
Dust furniture							
Dust light fixtures and switchplates							
Vacuum							
Tidy drawers							
Tidy bookshelves							
Empty Trash							
Declutter desk							
Clean out closet							
Discard old paperwork							

DAILY TASKS FOCUS	

SUPPLIES TO PURCHASE

Kids Chores

NAME: _____

CHORES	NUMBER OF TIMES						
	SUN	MON	TU	WED	THU	FRI	SAT

		NOTES

Cleaning Checklist

MONTH: _____

ADDITIONAL CLEANING	NUMBER OF TIMES						
	1	2	3	4	5	6	7

TASKS FOCUS	

SUPPLIES TO PURCHASE

Cleaning Checklist

MONTH: _____

KITCHEN	NUMBER OF TIMES						
	1	2	3	4	5	6	7
Mop							
Dust							
Wipe Cabinets							
Wipe Outside of Appliances							
Clean Inside of Microwave							
Clean Kitchen Sink							
Clean inside of refrigerator							
Clean inside of stove							
Dust light fixtures							
Clean blinds and curtains							
Wipe doors and baseboards							

DAILY TASKS FOCUS	
Wipe Counters & Stovetop	
Sweep	
Take out trash	
Do Dishes	

SUPPLIES TO PURCHASE

Cleaning Checklist

MONTH: _____

LIVING ROOM & DINNING ROOM	NUMBER OF TIMES						
	1	2	3	4	5	6	7
Vacuum							
Dust furniture							
Dust Pictures							
Dust light fixtures							
Clean blinds, curtains, drapes							
Clean inside windows							
Wipe windowsils							
Wipe baseboards & light switchplates							
Shampoo carpet							

DAILY TASKS FOCUS	
Clean up clutter	
Tidy magazines	
Fluff sofa pillows	

SUPPLIES TO PURCHASE

Cleaning Checklist

MONTH: _____

BATHROOM & LAUNDRY	1	2	3	4	5	6	7
Clean facebowl and counter							
Clean shower							
Wipe shower curtains/door							
Clean bathtub							
Clean mirrors & light fixtures							
Vacuum							
Mop							
Dust							
Wipe Cabinets & baseboards							
Empty trash							
Wash clothes							
Wash bedding							
Wash bath towels & cloths							

NUMBER OF TIMES

DAILY TASKS FOCUS	

SUPPLIES TO PURCHASE

Cleaning Checklist

MONTH: _____

BEDROOM	NUMBER OF TIMES						
	1	2	3	4	5	6	7
Make Beds							
Hang up clothes							
Fold and put away clothes							
Tidy room							
Dust furniture							
Dust light fixtures and switchplates							
Vacuum							
Tidy drawers							
Tidy bookshelves							
Empty Trash							
Declutter desk							
Clean out closet							
Discard old paperwork							

DAILY TASKS FOCUS

SUPPLIES TO PURCHASE

Cleaning Checklist

MONTH: _____

BEDROOM	NUMBER OF TIMES						
	1	2	3	4	5	6	7
Make Beds							
Hang up clothes							
Fold and put away clothes							
Tidy room							
Dust furniture							
Dust light fixtures and switchplates							
Vacuum							
Tidy drawers							
Tidy bookshelves							
Empty Trash							
Declutter desk							
Clean out closet							
Discard old paperwork							

DAILY TASKS FOCUS

SUPPLIES TO PURCHASE

Cleaning Checklist

BEDROOM	NUMBER OF TIMES						
	1	2	3	4	5	6	7
Make Beds							
Hang up clothes							
Fold and put away clothes							
Tidy room							
Dust furniture							
Dust light fixtures and switchplates							
Vacuum							
Tidy drawers							
Tidy bookshelves							
Empty Trash							
Declutter desk							
Clean out closet							
Discard old paperwork							

DAILY TASKS FOCUS	

SUPPLIES TO PURCHASE

Cleaning Checklist

MONTH: _____

BEDROOM	NUMBER OF TIMES						
	1	2	3	4	5	6	7
Make Beds							
Hang up clothes							
Fold and put away clothes							
Tidy room							
Dust furniture							
Dust light fixtures and switchplates							
Vacuum							
Tidy drawers							
Tidy bookshelves							
Empty Trash							
Declutter desk							
Clean out closet							
Discard old paperwork							

DAILY TASKS FOCUS	

SUPPLIES TO PURCHASE

Kids Chores

NAME: _____

CHORES	Number of Times						
	SUN	MON	TU	WED	THU	FRI	SAT

		NOTES

Cleaning Checklist

MONTH: _____

ADDITIONAL CLEANING	NUMBER OF TIMES						
	1	2	3	4	5	6	7

TASKS FOCUS

SUPPLIES TO PURCHASE

Cleaning Checklist

MONTH: _____

KITCHEN	NUMBER OF TIMES						
	1	2	3	4	5	6	7
Mop							
Dust							
Wipe Cabinets							
Wipe Outside of Appliances							
Clean Inside of Microwave							
Clean Kitchen Sink							
Clean inside of refrigerator							
Clean inside of stove							
Dust light fixtures							
Clean blinds and curtains							
Wipe doors and baseboards							

DAILY TASKS FOCUS	
Wipe Counters & Stovetop	
Sweep	
Take out trash	
Do Dishes	

SUPPLIES TO PURCHASE

Cleaning Checklist

MONTH: _____

LIVING ROOM & DINNING ROOM	NUMBER OF TIMES						
	1	2	3	4	5	6	7
Vacuum							
Dust furniture							
Dust Pictures							
Dust light fixtures							
Clean blinds, curtains, drapes							
Clean inside windows							
Wipe windowsils							
Wipe baseboards & light switchplates							
Shampoo carpet							

DAILY TASKS FOCUS	
Clean up clutter	
Tidy magazines	
Fluff sofa pillows	

SUPPLIES TO PURCHASE

Cleaning Checklist

MONTH: _____

BATHROOM & LAUNDRY	NUMBER OF TIMES						
	1	2	3	4	5	6	7
Clean facebowl and counter							
Clean shower							
Wipe shower curtains/door							
Clean bathtub							
Clean mirrors & light fixtures							
Vacuum							
Mop							
Dust							
Wipe Cabinets & baseboards							
Empty trash							
Wash clothes							
Wash bedding							
Wash bath towels & cloths							

DAILY TASKS FOCUS

SUPPLIES TO PURCHASE

Cleaning Checklist

MONTH: _____

BEDROOM	\multicolumn{7}{c}{NUMBER OF TIMES}						
	1	2	3	4	5	6	7
Make Beds							
Hang up clothes							
Fold and put away clothes							
Tidy room							
Dust furniture							
Dust light fixtures and switchplates							
Vacuum							
Tidy drawers							
Tidy bookshelves							
Empty Trash							
Declutter desk							
Clean out closet							
Discard old paperwork							

DAILY TASKS FOCUS

SUPPLIES TO PURCHASE

Cleaning Checklist

MONTH: _____

BEDROOM	NUMBER OF TIMES						
	1	2	3	4	5	6	7
Make Beds							
Hang up clothes							
Fold and put away clothes							
Tidy room							
Dust furniture							
Dust light fixtures and switchplates							
Vacuum							
Tidy drawers							
Tidy bookshelves							
Empty Trash							
Declutter desk							
Clean out closet							
Discard old paperwork							

DAILY TASKS FOCUS	

SUPPLIES TO PURCHASE

Cleaning Checklist

MONTH: _____

BEDROOM	NUMBER OF TIMES						
	1	2	3	4	5	6	7
Make Beds							
Hang up clothes							
Fold and put away clothes							
Tidy room							
Dust furniture							
Dust light fixtures and switchplates							
Vacuum							
Tidy drawers							
Tidy bookshelves							
Empty Trash							
Declutter desk							
Clean out closet							
Discard old paperwork							

DAILY TASKS FOCUS	

SUPPLIES TO PURCHASE

Cleaning Checklist

MONTH: _____

BEDROOM	NUMBER OF TIMES						
	1	2	3	4	5	6	7
Make Beds							
Hang up clothes							
Fold and put away clothes							
Tidy room							
Dust furniture							
Dust light fixtures and switchplates							
Vacuum							
Tidy drawers							
Tidy bookshelves							
Empty Trash							
Declutter desk							
Clean out closet							
Discard old paperwork							

DAILY TASKS FOCUS

SUPPLIES TO PURCHASE

Kids Chores

NAME: _____

CHORES	NUMBER OF TIMES						
	SUN	MON	TU	WED	THU	FRI	SAT

NOTES

Cleaning Checklist

MONTH: _____

ADDITIONAL CLEANING	NUMBER OF TIMES						
	1	2	3	4	5	6	7

TASKS FOCUS	

SUPPLIES TO PURCHASE

Cleaning Checklist

MONTH: _____

KITCHEN	NUMBER OF TIMES						
	1	2	3	4	5	6	7
Mop							
Dust							
Wipe Cabinets							
Wipe Outside of Appliances							
Clean Inside of Microwave							
Clean Kitchen Sink							
Clean inside of refrigerator							
Clean inside of stove							
Dust light fixtures							
Clean blinds and curtains							
Wipe doors and baseboards							

DAILY TASKS FOCUS	
Wipe Counters & Stovetop	
Sweep	
Take out trash	
Do Dishes	

SUPPLIES TO PURCHASE

Cleaning Checklist

MONTH: _____

LIVING ROOM & DINNING ROOM	NUMBER OF TIMES						
	1	2	3	4	5	6	7
Vacuum							
Dust furniture							
Dust Pictures							
Dust light fixtures							
Clean blinds, curtains, drapes							
Clean inside windows							
Wipe windowsils							
Wipe baseboards & light switchplates							
Shampoo carpet							

DAILY TASKS FOCUS	
Clean up clutter	
Tidy magazines	
Fluff sofa pillows	

SUPPLIES TO PURCHASE

Cleaning Checklist

MONTH: _____

BATHROOM & LAUNDRY	NUMBER OF TIMES						
	1	2	3	4	5	6	7
Clean facebowl and counter							
Clean shower							
Wipe shower curtains/door							
Clean bathtub							
Clean mirrors & light fixtures							
Vacuum							
Mop							
Dust							
Wipe Cabinets & baseboards							
Empty trash							
Wash clothes							
Wash bedding							
Wash bath towels & cloths							

DAILY TASKS FOCUS	

SUPPLIES TO PURCHASE

Cleaning Checklist

MONTH: _____

BEDROOM	NUMBER OF TIMES						
	1	2	3	4	5	6	7
Make Beds							
Hang up clothes							
Fold and put away clothes							
Tidy room							
Dust furniture							
Dust light fixtures and switchplates							
Vacuum							
Tidy drawers							
Tidy bookshelves							
Empty Trash							
Declutter desk							
Clean out closet							
Discard old paperwork							

DAILY TASKS FOCUS

SUPPLIES TO PURCHASE

Cleaning Checklist

MONTH: _____

BEDROOM	NUMBER OF TIMES						
	1	2	3	4	5	6	7
Make Beds							
Hang up clothes							
Fold and put away clothes							
Tidy room							
Dust furniture							
Dust light fixtures and switchplates							
Vacuum							
Tidy drawers							
Tidy bookshelves							
Empty Trash							
Declutter desk							
Clean out closet							
Discard old paperwork							

DAILY TASKS FOCUS

SUPPLIES TO PURCHASE

Cleaning Checklist

MONTH: _____

BEDROOM	NUMBER OF TIMES						
	1	2	3	4	5	6	7
Make Beds							
Hang up clothes							
Fold and put away clothes							
Tidy room							
Dust furniture							
Dust light fixtures and switchplates							
Vacuum							
Tidy drawers							
Tidy bookshelves							
Empty Trash							
Declutter desk							
Clean out closet							
Discard old paperwork							

DAILY TASKS FOCUS

SUPPLIES TO PURCHASE

Cleaning Checklist

MONTH: _____

BEDROOM	NUMBER OF TIMES						
	1	2	3	4	5	6	7
Make Beds							
Hang up clothes							
Fold and put away clothes							
Tidy room							
Dust furniture							
Dust light fixtures and switchplates							
Vacuum							
Tidy drawers							
Tidy bookshelves							
Empty Trash							
Declutter desk							
Clean out closet							
Discard old paperwork							

DAILY TASKS FOCUS

SUPPLIES TO PURCHASE

Kids Chores

NAME: _____

CHORES	SUN	MON	TU	WED	THU	FRI	SAT

NUMBER OF TIMES

NOTES

Cleaning Checklist

MONTH: _____

ADDITIONAL CLEANING	NUMBER OF TIMES						
	1	2	3	4	5	6	7

TASKS FOCUS	

SUPPLIES TO PURCHASE

Cleaning Checklist

MONTH: _____

KITCHEN	NUMBER OF TIMES						
	1	2	3	4	5	6	7
Mop							
Dust							
Wipe Cabinets							
Wipe Outside of Appliances							
Clean Inside of Microwave							
Clean Kitchen Sink							
Clean inside of refrigerator							
Clean inside of stove							
Dust light fixtures							
Clean blinds and curtains							
Wipe doors and baseboards							

DAILY TASKS FOCUS	
Wipe Counters & Stovetop	
Sweep	
Take out trash	
Do Dishes	

SUPPLIES TO PURCHASE

Cleaning Checklist

MONTH: _____

LIVING ROOM & DINNING ROOM	NUMBER OF TIMES						
	1	2	3	4	5	6	7
Vacuum							
Dust furniture							
Dust Pictures							
Dust light fixtures							
Clean blinds, curtains, drapes							
Clean inside windows							
Wipe windowsils							
Wipe baseboards & light switchplates							
Shampoo carpet							

DAILY TASKS FOCUS	
Clean up clutter	
Tidy magazines	
Fluff sofa pillows	

SUPPLIES TO PURCHASE

Cleaning Checklist

MONTH: _____

BATHROOM & LAUNDRY	NUMBER OF TIMES						
	1	2	3	4	5	6	7
Clean facebowl and counter							
Clean shower							
Wipe shower curtains/door							
Clean bathtub							
Clean mirrors & light fixtures							
Vacuum							
Mop							
Dust							
Wipe Cabinets & baseboards							
Empty trash							
Wash clothes							
Wash bedding							
Wash bath towels & cloths							

DAILY TASKS FOCUS

SUPPLIES TO PURCHASE

Cleaning Checklist

MONTH: _____

BEDROOM	NUMBER OF TIMES						
	1	2	3	4	5	6	7
Make Beds							
Hang up clothes							
Fold and put away clothes							
Tidy room							
Dust furniture							
Dust light fixtures and switchplates							
Vacuum							
Tidy drawers							
Tidy bookshelves							
Empty Trash							
Declutter desk							
Clean out closet							
Discard old paperwork							

DAILY TASKS FOCUS	

SUPPLIES TO PURCHASE

Cleaning Checklist

MONTH: _____

BEDROOM	NUMBER OF TIMES						
	1	2	3	4	5	6	7
Make Beds							
Hang up clothes							
Fold and put away clothes							
Tidy room							
Dust furniture							
Dust light fixtures and switchplates							
Vacuum							
Tidy drawers							
Tidy bookshelves							
Empty Trash							
Declutter desk							
Clean out closet							
Discard old paperwork							

DAILY TASKS FOCUS

SUPPLIES TO PURCHASE

Cleaning Checklist

MONTH: _____

BEDROOM	NUMBER OF TIMES						
	1	2	3	4	5	6	7
Make Beds							
Hang up clothes							
Fold and put away clothes							
Tidy room							
Dust furniture							
Dust light fixtures and switchplates							
Vacuum							
Tidy drawers							
Tidy bookshelves							
Empty Trash							
Declutter desk							
Clean out closet							
Discard old paperwork							

DAILY TASKS FOCUS	

SUPPLIES TO PURCHASE

Cleaning Checklist

MONTH: _____

BEDROOM	NUMBER OF TIMES						
	1	2	3	4	5	6	7
Make Beds							
Hang up clothes							
Fold and put away clothes							
Tidy room							
Dust furniture							
Dust light fixtures and switchplates							
Vacuum							
Tidy drawers							
Tidy bookshelves							
Empty Trash							
Declutter desk							
Clean out closet							
Discard old paperwork							

DAILY TASKS FOCUS	

SUPPLIES TO PURCHASE

Kids Chores

NAME: _____

CHORES	NUMBER OF TIMES						
	SUN	MON	TU	WED	THU	FRI	SAT

NOTES

Cleaning Checklist

MONTH: _____

ADDITIONAL CLEANING	NUMBER OF TIMES						
	1	2	3	4	5	6	7

TASKS FOCUS	

SUPPLIES TO PURCHASE

Cleaning Checklist

MONTH: _____

KITCHEN	NUMBER OF TIMES						
	1	2	3	4	5	6	7
Mop							
Dust							
Wipe Cabinets							
Wipe Outside of Appliances							
Clean Inside of Microwave							
Clean Kitchen Sink							
Clean inside of refrigerator							
Clean inside of stove							
Dust light fixtures							
Clean blinds and curtains							
Wipe doors and baseboards							

DAILY TASKS FOCUS	
Wipe Counters & Stovetop	
Sweep	
Take out trash	
Do Dishes	

SUPPLIES TO PURCHASE

Cleaning Checklist

MONTH: _____

LIVING ROOM & DINNING ROOM	NUMBER OF TIMES						
	1	2	3	4	5	6	7
Vacuum							
Dust furniture							
Dust Pictures							
Dust light fixtures							
Clean blinds, curtains, drapes							
Clean inside windows							
Wipe windowsils							
Wipe baseboards & light switchplates							
Shampoo carpet							

DAILY TASKS FOCUS	
Clean up clutter	
Tidy magazines	
Fluff sofa pillows	

SUPPLIES TO PURCHASE

Cleaning Checklist

MONTH: _____

BATHROOM & LAUNDRY	NUMBER OF TIMES						
	1	2	3	4	5	6	7
Clean facebowl and counter							
Clean shower							
Wipe shower curtains/door							
Clean bathtub							
Clean mirrors & light fixtures							
Vacuum							
Mop							
Dust							
Wipe Cabinets & baseboards							
Empty trash							
Wash clothes							
Wash bedding							
Wash bath towels & cloths							

DAILY TASKS FOCUS	

SUPPLIES TO PURCHASE

Cleaning Checklist

MONTH: _____

BEDROOM	NUMBER OF TIMES						
	1	2	3	4	5	6	7
Make Beds							
Hang up clothes							
Fold and put away clothes							
Tidy room							
Dust furniture							
Dust light fixtures and switchplates							
Vacuum							
Tidy drawers							
Tidy bookshelves							
Empty Trash							
Declutter desk							
Clean out closet							
Discard old paperwork							

DAILY TASKS FOCUS

SUPPLIES TO PURCHASE

Cleaning Checklist

MONTH: _____

BEDROOM	Number of Times						
	1	2	3	4	5	6	7
Make Beds							
Hang up clothes							
Fold and put away clothes							
Tidy room							
Dust furniture							
Dust light fixtures and switchplates							
Vacuum							
Tidy drawers							
Tidy bookshelves							
Empty Trash							
Declutter desk							
Clean out closet							
Discard old paperwork							

DAILY TASKS FOCUS

SUPPLIES TO PURCHASE

Cleaning Checklist

MONTH: _____

BEDROOM	NUMBER OF TIMES						
	1	2	3	4	5	6	7
Make Beds							
Hang up clothes							
Fold and put away clothes							
Tidy room							
Dust furniture							
Dust light fixtures and switchplates							
Vacuum							
Tidy drawers							
Tidy bookshelves							
Empty Trash							
Declutter desk							
Clean out closet							
Discard old paperwork							

DAILY TASKS FOCUS	

SUPPLIES TO PURCHASE

Cleaning Checklist

MONTH: _____

BEDROOM	NUMBER OF TIMES						
	1	2	3	4	5	6	7
Make Beds							
Hang up clothes							
Fold and put away clothes							
Tidy room							
Dust furniture							
Dust light fixtures and switchplates							
Vacuum							
Tidy drawers							
Tidy bookshelves							
Empty Trash							
Declutter desk							
Clean out closet							
Discard old paperwork							

DAILY TASKS FOCUS	

SUPPLIES TO PURCHASE

Kids Chores

NAME: _____

CHORES	NUMBER OF TIMES						
	SUN	MON	TU	WED	THU	FRI	SAT

NOTES

Cleaning Checklist

MONTH: _____

ADDITIONAL CLEANING	NUMBER OF TIMES						
	1	2	3	4	5	6	7

TASKS FOCUS	

SUPPLIES TO PURCHASE

Cleaning Checklist

MONTH: _____

OUTDOORS	NUMBER OF TIMES						
	1	2	3	4	5	6	7

FOCUS	

SUPPLIES TO PURCHASE

Made in the USA
Monee, IL
08 June 2023

35467269R00063